Dear *Grandma*
from you to me®

concept by Neil Coxon

from you to me®

© from you to me ltd 2010

Dear *Grandma*
from you to me®

This book is for your Grandmother's unique story.

It is for her to capture some of her life's key memories, experiences and feelings.

Ask her to complete it carefully and, if she wants to, add some photographs or images to personalize it more.

When it is finished and returned to you, this will be a record of her story . . . a story that you will treasure forever.

Dear

Here is a gift from me to you . . . for you to give to me.

When we are children we are always asking questions . . . well I now have some more for you.

Please answer them in the way that only you know how and then give the book back to me.

There might be a couple of questions that you prefer not to answer, so don't worry, just answer the others . . . I won't mind.

People say that we all have at least one book in us, and this will be yours.

The story of you and me that I will treasure forever.

Thank you,

with love

Tell me about the time and place you were born . . .

What are your earliest memories?

I'd like to know about your parents... names, dates of birth and tell me some stories about them...

Tell me what you know about your Mother's parents and family . . .

Tell me what you know about your Father's parents and family . . .

Please detail what you know of our family tree...

What **interesting** information do you know about other people in our family?

Here's some space for you to add more about our family that will **interest** generations to come . . .

What do you remember about the place/s you lived when you were a child?

What were your favorite childhood toys or games?

What kind of pets did you have when you were young and what were their names?

What do you remember about your vacations as a child?

What did you do for entertainment when you were young?

What did you study at school and what were you best at?

Tell me about the things you did as a child that are different for today's children . . .

What did you want to do when you grew up?

What were your favorite hobbies when you were young?

Did you have an idol when you were young?
Tell me who and why . . .

What was the first piece of music you bought?

What chores had to be done when you were young that aren't needed to be done today?

Describe any family traditions you had or maybe still have . . .

What age were you when you started work?
Tell me about the jobs you have had . . .

How did you meet my Grandfather?

What would you do for a night-out when you were dating?

Tell me about a special piece of music that you and my Grandfather had 'just for you'...

Describe your wedding . . .

Choosing the names for your children can be really difficult . . . how did you decide?

I would love to know more about my parents

. . . what can you tell me?

Tell me what my Mom or Dad was like when they were younger . . .

How did you feel when you were told you were going to be a grandparent?

What did you think when you first saw me after I was born?

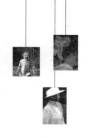

Can you see any characteristics in me that come from other people in our family?

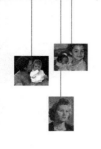

In what ways am I similar or different to my Mom or Dad?

Describe some of your favorite memories of the times we have spent together . . .

Describe what you **like** about me . . .

Is there anything you would like to change about me?

Tell me about the friends you have had in your life . . .

What piece/s of music would you choose in your own favorite 'top 10'?

Tell me about the **furthest** place you have **traveled** to . . .

What are the happiest or greatest memories of your life?

What are a few of your favorite things?

Describe your memory of some major world events that have happened in your lifetime . . .

Describe the greatest change that you have seen in your lifetime so far . . .

Do you think life today is **better** or **worse** than when you were young? How is it *different*?

Who or what has been the greatest influence on you?

If you were an animal... what type of animal would you be, and why?

If you won the Lottery... what would you do with the money?

What have you found most difficult in your life?

What is your biggest regret in your life?

Can you do anything about it now?

Tell me about the things that have made you happy or laugh...

With hindsight what would you do differently?

Describe something you still want to achieve in your life . . .

Tell me something you think I won't know about you . . .

What would you like your epitaph to say?

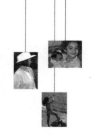

Given your experiences, what advice would you like to offer me?

And now your chance to tell me some other **personal stories** that you want to share . . .

These extra pages are for us to write any **questions, memories** or **answers** that may not have been covered elsewhere in the book . . .

And finally for the record . . .

what is your full name ?

what was your maiden name ?

what is your date of birth ?

what color are your eyes ?

how tall are you ?

what blood group are you ?

what was the date when you completed this story for me ?

Dear

I will treasure this book, your memories and your advice forever.

I hope you enjoyed answering my questions.

Thank you so much for doing it and for writing your own book about you and me . . .

from you to me

Dear Grandma

from you to me®

First published in the UK by *from you to me*, February 2007
US version - July 2010
Copyright, *from you to me* limited 2010
Hackless House, Murhill, Bath, BA2 7FH, UK
www.fromyoutome.com
E-mail: hello@fromyoutome.com

ISBN 978-1-907048-31-9

Cover design by so design consultants, Wick, Bristol, UK
Printed and bound in the UK by CPI William Clowes, Beccles

This paper is manufactured from material sourced from forests certified according to strict environmental, social and economical standards.

If you think other questions should be included in future editions, please let us know. And please share some of the interesting answers you receive with us at the *from you to me* website to let other people read about these fascinating insights . . .

If you liked the concept of this book, please tell your family and friends and look out for others in the *from you to me* range:

Dear Mom, from you to me
Dear Dad, from you to me
Dear Grandpa, from you to me
Dear Sister, from you to me
Dear Brother, from you to me
Dear Son, from you to me
Dear Daughter, from you to me

Dear Friend, from you to me
Digging up Memories, from you to me
Cooking up Memories, from you to me
These were the days, from you to me
Christmas Present, Christmas Past, from you to me
other relationship and memory journals available soon . . .

You can also create your own personalized version at www.fromyoutome.com

All rights reserved. No part of this publication may be reproduced, stored in a retrieval system or transmitted in any form or by any means, electronic, mechanical, photocopying or otherwise circulated without the publisher's prior consent in any form of binding or cover other than that in which it is published and without a similar condition including this.